W9-CLQ-176

To:

_____

From:

_____

BB

Brighton Books
Nashville, TN

A Woman's Journey...
With God

A Woman's Journey... With God

*A celebration of the Christian life
from childhood to maturity*

By Mary Prince

Table of Contents

BRIGHTON BOOKS
Nashville, TN 37204

ISBN 1-58334-123-4

The quoted ideas expressed in this book (but not scripture verses) are not, in all cases, exact quotations, as some have been edited for clarity and brevity. In all cases, the author has attempted to maintain the speaker's original intent. In some cases, quoted material for this book was obtained from secondary sources, primarily print media. While every effort was made to ensure the accuracy of these sources, the accuracy cannot be guaranteed. For additions, deletions, corrections or clarifications in future editions of this text, please write BRIGHTON BOOKS.

All scripture quotations, unless otherwise indicated, are taken from the HOLY BIBLE, NEW INTERNATIONAL VERSION ©. NIV ©. Copyright © 1973, 1978, 1984, by International Bible Society. Used by permission of Zondervan Publishing House. All rights reserved.

Scripture taken from *THE MESSAGE*. Copyright © 1993, 1994,1995,1996. Used by permission of NavPress Publishing Group.

Scripture taken from the NEW AMERICAN STANDARD BIBLE®, Copyright © 1960, 1962, 1963, 1968, 1971, 1972, 1973, 1975, 1977, 1995 by The Lockman Foundation. Used by permission.

Scripture quotations marked (NLT) are taken from The Holy Bible, New Living Translation, Copyright © 1996. Used by permission of Tyndale House Publishers, Incorporated, Wheaton, Illinois 60189. All rights reserved.

Printed in the United States of America
Cover Design & Page Layout: *Bart Dawson*

1 2 3 4 5 6 7 8 9 10 • 01 02 03 04 05 06 07 08 09 10

Acknowledgments: The author is indebted to Criswell Freeman for his support and friendship, to Bonnie DeArmond for her tireless consultation and research on this book, and to the helpful staff at Walnut Grove Press.

To Eloise Gallery and Mary James,

Extraordinary Women

I want to know Christ

and the power of his resurrection...

Not that I have already obtained

all this, or have already been

made perfect, but I press on

to take hold of that for which

Christ Jesus took hold of me....

Philippians 3:10,12

Introduction

*L*ike most people, I enjoy taking trips. Visiting new places and revisiting old ones adds excitement and wonderment to my life. I enjoy traveling to parks and forests to view God's glorious creation, and I delight in trips to historical places where I can learn more about the history of the world we live in. But most of all, I savor trips that allow me to spend time with my family and friends. On these occasions, the importance of the destination is secondary to the quality of the time we spend together. When we travel life's roads with those we love, the point of destination is always secondary to the quality of the journey.

In life, every journey has wonderful, unexpected serendipities which have the potential to enrich us. If, as we travel, we slow ourselves down long enough to savor the scenery, we will surely discover unexpected treasures. But, if we allow ourselves to be hurried and harried, we will just as surely miss the wondrous details of God's creation, thus robbing ourselves of the joy and insight that God intends for our lives.

Sometimes, as we travel life's road, unanticipated difficulties arise. If we allow God to meet us in these difficulties, He will protect us, He will teach us, He will affirm us, and He will transform us. No matter our destination, no matter our circumstances, God travels with us. But the defining question of our lives is this: Will *we* travel with God?

This book is about a woman's journey with God. The ultimate destination of that journey is not of this earth; it is, of course, the eternal life that God promises His children. As the old hymn reminds us, this world is not our home…we're just passing through. But pass through it we must, and the quality of life's journey is dependent, first and forever, upon the quality of our relationship with the ultimate traveling companion: our Creator.

Sometimes, we find ourselves on the mountaintop, enjoying breathtaking vistas. Other times, we find ourselves in the valley with no view of the horizon. Good times and bad times are all part of the tapestry of each human life, but even in our darkest hours, we can be comforted: Wherever life leads us, God was there first — and He's still there, waiting to lead us back to the mountaintop…*His* mountaintop….if we only take His hand and begin the journey.

Chapter 1

A Journey of Trust

Trust in the LORD with all your heart
and lean not on your own understanding....

—

Proverbs 3:5

Most children are very trusting by nature. We adults encourage that trust with a game: As the child stands on the edge of the bed (or at the edge of the pool), we beckon him or her to jump into our waiting arms. When children hesitate, we assure them that we are trustworthy. Then, when they squeal with delight and jump, we catch them and applaud their courage and trust in us.

As adults, we, too, must play a game of trust. Throughout life, we are called upon to trust God's will and His plans for His children. Of course, life's journey has a way of taking unanticipated turns; many times these turns make no sense to us. Life can be unpredictable, fear-provoking, and, at times, tear-provoking; yet, in our darkest moments, when we are incapable of fully understanding God's plan for our lives, we must trust Him.

God calls upon us to make countless "leaps of faith," even when we are uncertain or afraid. Like timid children, we stand at the edge, hearing God's Word yet afraid to respond. But, if we trust our Lord and answer His call, we are protected. Like the loving Father that He is, God beckons us to make a leap of faith and to trust Him. Then, He stands beside us, patiently, until we jump — and when we do, He catches us lovingly in His waiting arms.

Never be afraid to trust an unknown future
to a known God.

Corrie ten Boom

Sometimes when I was a child
my mother or father would say,
"Shut your eyes and hold out your hand."
That was the promise of some lovely surprise.
I trusted them so I shut my eyes instantly
and held out my hand. Whatever they
were going to give me I was ready to take.
So it should be in our trust of our heavenly Father.
Faith is the willingness to receive whatever
He wants to give or the willingness not to have
what He does not want to give.

Elisabeth Elliot

In God, whose word I praise,

in God I trust;

I will not be afraid.

Psalm 56:4

Either we are adrift in chaos or we are individuals,
created, loved, upheld and placed purposefully,
exactly where we are. Can you believe that?
Can you trust God for that?

Elisabeth Elliot

You will be able to trust Him only
to the extent that you know Him!

Kay Arthur

When the train goes through a tunnel
and the world gets dark, do you jump out?
Of course not. You sit still
and trust the engineer to get you through.

Corrie ten Boom

It is better to take refuge in the Lord than to trust in man. It is better to take refuge in the Lord than to trust in princes.

Psalm 118:8,9

If my life is surrendered to God, all is well.
    Let me not grab it back, as though it were
    in peril in His hand but would be safer in mine!

Elisabeth Elliot

The act of thanksgiving is a demonstration of
    the fact that you are going to trust
    and believe God.

Kay Arthur

Cast your cares on the Lord

and he will sustain you....

Psalm 55:22

Chapter 2

A Journey of Security

Holy Father, protect them by the power
of your name—the name you gave me....

—

Jesus
John 17:11

A little girl's father had been seriously injured in an accident and was in the hospital. The girl was anxious and worried at bedtime, so she asked her mother if she could sleep with her. In the darkness of the room, the little girl asked, "Mommy, is your face turned towards me?" Her mother responded, "Yes," and soon the mother could hear the rhythmic, peaceful breathing of a little girl asleep. Then, the mother quietly slipped from bed and went to the window. She looked to the sky and asked, "Father, is your face turned toward me?"

Sometimes, God seems so very near, but other times, we experience uncertainty and insecurity as we face challenges that sap our strength and test our faith. In times of trouble, we are challenged to remember that the only true security is found in God through Jesus Christ. And how comforting it is to know that the Father's face is, indeed, always turned toward us.

Submit each day to God, knowing that He
is God over all your tomorrows.

Kay Arthur

There is no fear in love;
but perfect love casts out fear.

John 4:18

...if a person fears God, he or she has no reason
to fear anything else. On the other hand,
if a person does not fear God, then
fear becomes a way of life.

Beth Moore

...If God is for us, who can be against us?

Paul

Romans 8:31

So, what do you think?
    With God on our side like this, how can we lose?
        If God didn't hesitate to put everything
      on the line for us, embracing our condition
        and exposing himself to the worst
    by sending his own Son, is there anything else
        He wouldn't gladly and freely do for us?

Paul

Romans 8:31,32 The Message

Weave the unveiling fabric of God's word
   through your heart and mind.
It will hold strong, even if the rest of life unravels.

Gigi Graham Tchividjian

Nothing happens by happenstance.
 I am not in the hands of fate, nor am I the victim
   of man's whims or the devil's ploys.
   There is One who sits above man,
  above Satan, and above all heavenly hosts
 as the ultimate authority of all the universe.
   That One is my God and my Father.

Kay Arthur

Love is the seed of all hope.
   It is the enticement to trust,
    to risk, to try, to go on.

Gloria Gaither

Oh yes, you shaped me first inside, then out;
    you formed me in my mother's womb.
I thank you, High God—you're breathtaking!
    Body and soul, I am marvelously made!
    I worship in adoration—
    what a creation!
You know me inside and out,
    you know every bone in my body;
You know exactly how I was made, bit by bit,
    how I was sculpted from nothing into
    something.
Like an open book, you watched me grow from
    conception to birth; all the stages of
    my life were spread out before you,
The days of my life all prepared
    before I'd even lived one day.

Psalm 139:13-16 The Message

Don't be overwhelmed...

take it one day and

one prayer at a time.

Stormie Omartian

Even before God created the heavens and the earth.
He knew you and me, *and He chose us!*
You and I were born because it was
God's good pleasure.

Kay Arthur

For he chose us in him before the creation
of the world to be holy and blameless in his sight.
In love he predestined us to be adopted
as his sons through Jesus Christ,
in accordance with his pleasure and will....

Paul
Ephesians 1:4,5

Not a star, not a planet, not a meteorite or a quasar,
no, not even a black hole is missing.
God made them. He knows their names,
knows exactly where they belong.
Can He keep track of us?

Elisabeth Elliot

...because God is my sovereign Lord,
I was not worried. He manages perfectly,
day and night, year in and year out, the movements
of the stars, the wheeling of the planets,
the staggering coordination of events
that goes on the molecular level in order to
hold things together. There is no doubt that
He can manage the timing of my days and weeks.

Elisabeth Elliot

We have this hope as an anchor for the soul, firm
and secure. It enters the inner sanctuary behind
the curtain, where Jesus, who went before us,
has entered on our behalf. He has become
a high priest forever, in the order of Melchizedek.

Hebrews 6:19,20

Worry is a cycle of inefficient thoughts whirling around a center of fear.

Corrie ten Boom

Chapter 3

A Journey of Awe and Wonder

For the LORD your God is God of gods and Lord of lords, the great God, mighty and awesome.

—

Deuteronomy 10:17

Children have a tremendous capacity to be amazed and delighted by the simple wonders of life. A baby carefully examines her toes and fingers; a child laughs in amazement as she chases bubbles around the yard; a child is thrilled by the antics of a little kitten; a baby is enchanted by the colorful, musical mobile hanging above the crib; and the list goes on.

Jesus says, *"I tell you the truth, unless you change and become like little children, you will never enter the kingdom of heaven. Therefore, whoever humbles himself like this child is the greatest in the kingdom of heaven."(Matthew 18:3,4)* We know that God's universe is wondrous to behold, and when we pause to consider the beauty of a sunset or the majesty of a clear, starry night, we are awed. Sometimes, the demands of everyday life cause us to become preoccupied, and sometimes we fail to appreciate the miracle of God's handiwork. When we find ourselves caught in the trap of the daily grind, we must stop, be still, and ask God to restore our sense of wonderment. Then, with a renewed sense of perspective, we — like our children — can see the hand of God in every miraculous fiber of His creation.

You answer us with awesome deeds

of righteousness, O God

our Savior... Those living far away

fear your wonders; where morning dawns

and evening fades

you call forth songs of joy.

Psalm 65:5,8

...we will stand amazed to see the topside
of the tapestry and how God beautifully
embroidered each circumstance into a pattern
for our good and His glory.

Joni Eareckson Tada

Knowing God's sovereignty and unconditional love
imparts a beauty to life...and to you.

Kay Arthur

He created us because He delights in us.

Beth Moore

Take a good look at God's wonders;

they'll take your breath away.

He converted sea to dry land;

travelers crossed the river on foot.

Now isn't that cause for a song?

Psalm 66:5,6 *The Message*

In Biblical worship, you do not find the repetition
of a phrase; instead, you find the worshipers
rehearsing the character of God and His ways,
reminding Him of His faithfulness
and His wonderful promises.

Kay Arthur

Preoccupy my thoughts with
Your praise beginning today.

Prayer by Joni Eareckson Tada

How do you wait upon the Lord?
First you must learn to sit at His feet
and take time to listen to His words.

Kay Arthur

Whence comes this idea that if what we are doing
is fun, it can't be God's will? The God who made
giraffes, a baby's fingernails, a puppy's tail,
a crooknecked squash, the bobwhite's call,
and a young girl's giggle, has a sense of humor.
Make no mistake about that.

Catherine Marshall

The God who created names and numbers and
the stars in the heavens also numbers the hairs
of my head. . . . He pays attention to very big things
and to very small ones. What matters to me
matters to Him, and that changes my life.

Elisabeth Elliot

You are awesome, O God, in your sanctuary;
the God of Israel gives power
and strength to his people.
Praise be to God.

Psalm 68:35

In the sanctuary, we discover beauty:
the beauty of His presence.

Kay Arthur

Chapter 4

A Journey of Freedom

...you will know the truth,
and the truth will set you free.

—

Jesus
John 8:32

*A*re you tired? Worn out? Burned out on religion? Come to me. Get away with me and you'll recover your life. I'll show you how to take a real rest. Walk with me and work with me—watch how I do it. Learn the unforced rhythms of grace. I won't lay anything ill-fitting on you. Keep company with me and you'll learn to live freely and lightly. *(Matthew 11:28-30 The Message)*

Jesus bids us to walk with Him. Our walk with Him is not without struggles, and it is not without sufferings, but Jesus promises that even in the midst of our travails, we can live freely and lightly if we choose to journey with Him. The choice is ours: We can either place ourselves in the service of a benevolent Christ and, in doing so, find freedom, or we can seek to live outside God's will for our lives…and suffer the inevitable consequences.

The Christ-centered life fits us and makes us graceful. When we *keep company* with Jesus, He promises us that we will not only *recover* our lives but also that we will be free. The demands of the world are exhausting, but the mantle of Christ is energizing. As believers, we can bear that mantle with a sense of thanksgiving and peace.

Are you tired? Worn out? Bitter? Saddened? Afraid? Take your very next step with Jesus at your side. You'll find energy and grace and freedom and peace, now and forever.

The God who orchestrates the universe has
a good many things to consider that have not
occurred to me, and it is well
that I leave them to Him.

Elisabeth Elliot

If your every human plan and calculation has
miscarried—if, one by one, human props have been
knocked out…take heart. God is trying to get a
message through to you, and the message is:
"Stop depending on inadequate human resources.
Let me handle the matter."

Catherine Marshall

Really, then, our problem is not weakness,
but independence! And in covenant,
you die to independent living.

Kay Arthur

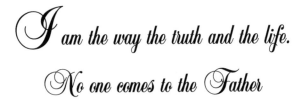

I am the way the truth and the life.
No one comes to the *Father*

but through me.

Jesus
John 14:6

Those who walk in truth walk in liberty.

Beth Moore

It is not my ability, but my response
to God's ability that counts.

Corrie ten Boom

When trials come your way—as inevitably they will—
do not run away.
Run to your God and Father.

Kay Arthur

...let us throw off everything that hinders
and the sin that so easily entangles,
and let us run with perseverance
the race marked out for us.

Hebrews 12:1

When we are set free from the bondage
of pleasing others, when we are free from currying
others' favor and others' approval—then no one
will be able to make us miserable or dissatisfied.
And then, if we know we have pleased God,
contentment will be our consolation.

Kay Arthur

Christians see sin for what it is: willful rebellion against the rulership of God in their lives. And in turning from their sin, they have embraced God's only means of dealing with sin: Jesus.

Kay Arthur

As a child of God,

you are no longer a slave to sin.

Kay Arthur

Chapter 5
A Journey of Strength

I love you, O LORD, my strength.

—

Psalm 18:1

She had been through so much, and now her husband was gone. All strength and willpower had been drained from every part of her being. All she could do was pray, "Lord, give me the strength to cross the street." Her only empowering scripture was, *Give me today my daily bread. (Matthew 6:11)* She needed not only physical sustenance but also emotional, spiritual, and mental strength.

The twists and turns of life's journey will sometimes leave us devastated. In our darkest moments, we may feel as though we are without the strength to take another step. All doors seem closed to us, and all hope seems lost to us. During these times, the encouragement of friends and family — even the most well-intentioned — may fail to lift our spirits. Sermons, songs, and self-help books may not have the ability to move us. But the Lord does.

In our weakness, God empowers. In our moments of doubt, God assures. When we fall, He lifts us up, and when we weep, He dries our tears. God gives freely to those who call upon Him. He is waiting patiently to provide us with His life-giving power. Our task is to ask God to share His infinite strength; His promise is that He will.

It is as we come to the Lord in our nothingness, our powerlessness, our helplessness that He then enables us to love in a way which would be absolutely impossible without Him.

Elisabeth Elliot

Worry does not empty tomorrow of its sorrow;
        it empties today of its strength.

Corrie ten Boom

But seek first his kingdom and his righteousness
        and all these things will be given to you as well.
            Therefore do not worry about tomorrow,
                for tomorrow will worry about itself.
            Each day has enough trouble of its own.

Jesus
Matthew 6:33,34

I lived with Indians who made pots out of clay,
which they used for cooking. Nobody was interested
in the pot. Everybody was interested in what
was inside. The same clay taken out of the same
riverbed, always made in the same design,
nothing special about it. Well, I'm a clay pot
and let me not forget it. But the excellency
of the power is of God and not us.

Elisabeth Elliot

Yet, O LORD, you are our Father.
We are the clay, you are the potter;
we are all the work of your hand.

Isaiah 64:8

My grace is sufficient for you,
for my power is made perfect in weakness.

2 Corinthians 12:9

We are never stronger than the moment
we admit we are weak.

Beth Moore

But I will sing of your strength,

in the morning I will sing of your love;

for you are my fortress,

my refuge in times of trouble.

Psalm 59:16

Proclaim the power of God,

whose majesty is over Israel,

whose power is in the skies.

You are awesome, O God,

in your sanctuary;

the God of Israel gives

power and strength to his people.

Praise be to God!

Psalm 68:34,35

Chapter 6

A Journey of Refreshment

...inwardly we are being renewed day by day.

—

2 Corinthians 4:16

Elijah had just experienced one of the greatest victories recorded in the Bible. He had challenged hundreds of the prophets of Baal on Mount Carmel, and Elijah the prophet of God, had won decisively. One might expect that a great celebration would ensue and that Elijah would have enjoyed the spotlight. Instead, we read that Elijah fled into the desert where he prayed that God might take his life. Elijah went from the glory on the mountaintop to the despair of the valley in a single day. *(I Kings 18)*

Sometimes, we, like Elijah, suffer changes of attitude that leave us discouraged or worse. During such times, we need what God provided Elijah: refreshment. First, God gave Elijah sleep and rest under the shade of a tree. Then, an angel appeared with hot bread and a jar of water. Soon, more sleep and more food was supplied by God, and eventually Elijah's strength and courage was restored. *(1 Kings 19)*

Wherever we find ourselves in life, whether we are victorious or vanquished, triumphant or troubled, we can discover refreshment in the comfort of God's Holy Spirit. When we encounter those inevitable desert experiences, those times when the mountaintop seems so far away, God can refresh us. Jesus, Paul, and Moses experienced their times in the desert, and all experienced God's renewal of their lives and their work. We, too, can depend upon God to restore our souls and to refresh our spirits as we seek His will and accept His peace.

Create in me a pure heart, O God,
      and renew a steadfast spirit within me.
Do not cast me from your presence
      or take your Holy Spirit from me.
Restore to me the joy of your salvation
      and grant me a willing spirit, to sustain me.

King David
Psalm 51:10-12

Soak me in your laundry and I'll come out clean,
      Scrub me and I'll have a snow-white life.
Tune me in to foot-tapping songs,
      Set these once-broken bones to dancing.
Don't look too close for blemishes,
      Give me a clean bill of health.
God, make a fresh start in me,
      Shape a Genesis week from the chaos
      of my life.

King David
Psalm 51:10-12 The Message

Unparalleled joy and victory come
from allowing Christ to do "the hard thing" with us.

Beth Moore

This hard place in which you perhaps find yourself
is the very place in which God is giving you
opportunity to look only to Him, to spend time in
prayer, and to learn long-suffering gentleness and
meekness—in short, to learn the depths of the love
that Christ Himself has poured out on all of us.

Elisabeth Elliot

...being confident of this, that he who began

a good work in you will carry it on to

completion until the day of Christ Jesus.

Paul
Philippians 1:6

For you, O God, tested us;

you refined us like silver.

You brought us into prison

and laid burdens on our backs.

You let men ride over our heads;

we went through fire and water,

but you brought us to a place of abundance.

Psalm 66:10-12

Even in the winter, even in the midst of the storm,
the sun is still there. Somewhere, up above
the clouds, it still shines and warms and pulls at
the life buried deep inside the brown branches
and frozen earth. The sun is there!
Spring will come.

Gloria Gaither

Let's never forget that some of God's
greatest mercies are His refusals.
He says no in order that He may, in some way we
cannot imagine, say yes. All His ways with us are
merciful. His meaning is always love.

Elisabeth Elliot

Are you weak? Weary? Confused? Troubled?
Pressured? How is your relationship with God?
Is it held in its place of priority? I believe
the greater the pressure, the greater your need
for time alone with Him.

Kay Arthur

God walks with us. . . .
He scoops us up in His arms or simply sits with us
in silent strength until we cannot avoid the awesome
recognition that yes, even now, He is there.

Gloria Gaither

Snuggle in God's arms. When you are hurting,
when you feel lonely, left out. . .
let Him cradle you, comfort you, reassure you
of His all-sufficient power and love.

Kay Arthur

He is the God of wholeness and restoration.

Stormie Omartian

In essence, my testimony is that there is life
after failure. Abundant, effective, spirit-filled life…
for those who are willing to repent hard
and work hard.

Beth Moore

Often God shuts a door in our face
so that He can open the door
through which He wants us to go.

Catherine Marshall

When things happen which dismay, we ought to look
to God for His meaning, and remember that
He is not taken by surprise nor can
His purposes be thwarted in the end.

Elisabeth Elliot

Be good to me, God—and now!
I've run to you for dear life.
I'm hiding out under your wings
until the hurricane blows over.

Psalm 57:1 The Message

He created us because He delights in us.

Beth Moore

...it is God who works in you to do His will
and to act according to his good purpose.

Philippians 2:13

God has no problems, only plans.

Corrie ten Boom

Chapter 7
A Journey of Certainty

…I know whom I have believed, and am convinced
that He is able to guard what I have entrusted
to Him for that day.

—

2 Timothy 1:12

I once heard a radio speaker testify that since Jesus came into his life, the man had never had a scintilla of doubt about God. I doubt it. When Jesus comes into our lives, He goes to work recreating us in the image of God. That means we haven't yet arrived. In other words, we mortals, being incomplete and imperfect, are subject to doubt.

John the Baptist, while still in his mother's womb, sensed the presence of Jesus when a pregnant Mary approached: *When Elizabeth heard Mary's greeting, the baby leaped in her womb….(Luke 1:41)* John the Baptist proclaimed Jesus as he preached in the wilderness: *Prepare the way for the Lord, make straight paths for him. (Luke 3:4)* And John the Baptist knew Jesus was the Son of God when Jesus approached him to be baptized: *I need to be baptized by you and do you come to me?" (Matthew 3:14)* Yet, near the end of his life, while in prison, John the Baptist sent messengers to Jesus to ask, *Are you the one who was to come, or should we expect someone else? (Matthew 11:2)*

Even John the Baptist had doubts, and that's okay. The important element of this story is that John the Baptist took his doubts to Jesus. So should we.

All of us, like John the Baptist, experience times of uncertainty. When we take our questions to Jesus, He responds as He did to John the Baptist: *Go back and report to John what you hear and see: The blind receive sight, the lame walk, those who have leprosy are cured, the deaf hear, the dead are raised, and the good news is preached to the poor.* (Matthew 11:4,5) Jesus provided John with the certainty he needed, and Jesus will do the same for believers of every age.

When our journeys leave us with more questions than answers, we can take our doubts to Jesus in prayer. Then, Jesus — in His own way and in His own time — can replace those doubts with a confident assurance of God's promises and a peaceful acceptance of God's will.

And with the mind of Christ we shall "know fully."
While we were on earth…we scratched our heads
and wondered how the matted mesh of threads
in Romans 8:28 could possibly be woven together
for our good.

Joni Eareckson Tada

And we know that in all things God works
for the good of those who love him,
who have been called according to his purpose.

Romans 8:28

I do know that waiting on God requires the willingness to bear uncertainty, to carry within oneself the unanswered question, lifting the heart to God about it whenever it intrudes upon one's thoughts. It is easy to talk oneself into a decision that has no permanence — easier sometimes than to wait patiently.

Elisabeth Elliot

God's curriculum for all who sincerely want
to know Him and do His will always includes lessons
we wish we could skip. . . . With intimate
understanding of our deepest needs and individual
capacities, He chooses our curriculum.

Elisabeth Elliot

How often it occurs to me, as it must to you,
that it is far easier simply to cooperate with God!

Beth Moore

Christ knows better than you what it means
to be human.

Joni Eareckson Tada

For I gave them the words you gave

me and they accepted them.

They knew with certainty that

I came from you, and they believed

that you sent me.

Jesus
John 17:8

Now we see but a poor reflection

as in a mirror; then

we shall see face to face.

Now I know in part;

then I shall know fully,

even as I am fully known.

1 Corinthians 13:12

Don't worry about what you do not understand....
Worry about what you do understand in
the Bible but do not live by.

Corrie ten Boom

I'm convinced that there is nothing that can happen
to me in this life that is not precisely designed
by a sovereign Lord to give me the opportunity
to learn to know Him.

Elisabeth Elliot

There may be no trumpet sound or loud applause
when we make a right decision, just a calm sense
of resolution and peace.

Gloria Gaither

We will never cease to need
our Father – His wisdom,
direction, help, and support.
We will never outgrow Him.
We will always need His grace.

Kay Arthur

Chapter 8
A Journey of Contentment

...I have learned to be content whatever
the circumstances.

—

Paul
Philippians 4:11

The little girl enjoyed the bright sunshine as she played in the ocean with her dad. She sat on the raft while her father swam along beside. When the father discovered how far they had traveled from the shore, it was too late. The current was so strong he could not swim and pull the raft back to the safety of the shoreline. So he told his little girl to stay still on the raft, and he assured her that he would return very quickly to get her.

The current was much stronger than the father anticipated, and his struggle to reach shore took much longer than he had hoped. Once ashore, he found a sheriff's patrol boat and returned to his daughter. The girl was a little sunburned, but remarkably calm and composed. When asked by the sheriff's deputy how she remained so calm, she replied, "I wasn't worried. I knew my father was coming back."

Much of our contentment in this expedition called life is based on our belief in our heavenly Father and His promises. We may experience times of aloneness, and we may suffer through anxious moments, but as Christians, we need never lose hope. Our hope springs from our belief in God and in His purposes toward us.

Our lives change, our circumstances change, and the world changes, but God remains unchanged. He is *the same yesterday and today and forever. (Hebrews 13:8)* No matter where the currents of life may lead us, no matter how far we may drift, we can be content in the knowledge that we are safe in the arms of an unchanging God. Our Father has promised us protection and salvation. And He always keeps His promises.

I'm just as happy with little as with much, with much as with little. I've found the recipe for being happy whether full or hungry, hands full or hands empty. Whatever I have, wherever I am, I can make it through anything in the One who makes me who I am.

Paul
Philippians 4:12-13 The Message

Everything I possess of any worth
is a direct product of God's love.

Beth Moore

If we just give God the little that we have,
we can trust Him to make it go around.

Gloria Gaither

I have held many things in my hands,
and I have lost them all;
but whatever I have placed in God's hands,
that I still possess.

Corrie Ten Boom

If we know we have pleased God,
contentment will be our consolation,
for what pleases God will please us.

Kay Arthur

…get ready for God to show you not only His pleasure,
but His approval.

Joni Eareckson Tada

Make God's will the focus of your life day by day.
If you seek to please Him and Him alone,
you'll find yourself satisfied with life.

Kay Arthur

So we make it our goal to please him….

2 Corinthians 5:9

Whom have I in heaven but you?
And earth has nothing I desire
besides you. My flesh
and my heart may fail,
but God is the strength
of my heart...forever.

Psalm 73:25,26

We are women,

and my plea is let me be a woman,

holy through and through,

asking for nothing but what God wants

to give me, receiving with both hands

and with all my heart whatever that is.

Elisabeth Elliot

I've learned to hold everything loosely because
   it hurts when God pries my fingers from it.

Corrie ten Boom

Acceptance says, true, this is my situation
   at the moment. I'll look unblinkingly at
the reality of it. But I'll also open my hands
      to accept willingly whatever
      a loving Father sends me.

Catherine Marshall

For we are God's workmanship,
    created in Christ Jesus to do good works,
    which God prepared in advance for us to do.

Ephesians 2:10

I thank you for the knowledge that I give
    you pleasure when I follow your ways.

Prayer by Joni Eareckson Tada

...Measure the size of the obstacles
against the size of God.

Beth Moore

No giant will ever be a match for a big God
with a little rock.

Beth Moore

David said to the Philistine,
"You come against me with sword and spear
and javelin, but I come against you
in the name of the LORD Almighty...."

1 Samuel 17:45

Rejoicing is a matter of obedience
to God – an obedience that will start you
on the road to peace and contentment.

Kay Arthur

Chapter 9

A Journey of Change

...I consider everything a loss compared to
the surpassing greatness of knowing
Christ Jesus my Lord....

—

Paul
Philippians 3:8

*L*ife is an unfolding series of changes. Some changes we bring about ourselves, and some changes are thrust upon us. Some changes are easy to accept, while others are hard. Sometimes, the adjustments we must make are gradual, expected, and benign. But sometimes in life, dramatic, unpleasant adjustments must be made whether we like it or not.

All of us enjoy our zones of comfort. When life allows us continuity and constancy, we tend to feel reassured that all is right with the world. But when circumstances present us with unwelcome changes, the world may seem to be a threatening place indeed. When the winds of change seem ominous, we, as Christians, can be comforted in the firm knowledge that God is still at work in our lives, molding and shaping us.

Keep your eyes on Jesus, who both began and finished this race we're in. Study how he did it. Because he never lost sight of where he was headed—that exhilarating finish in and with God—he could put up with anything along the way: cross, shame, whatever. (Hebrews 12:2 The Message) Life's inevitable changes are put into perspective when we focus upon our Lord. Any loss can be turned into a gain with Jesus. Of course, the world is in a state of constant change, as are we. God is not. Through good times and bad, through happiness and sorrow, through all the unending changes that are the hallmark of every human life, God is still God, and He will sustain.

If you are God's child, you are no longer bound
to your past or to what you were.
You are a brand new creature in Christ Jesus.

Kay Arthur

Therefore, if anyone is in Christ, he is a new creation;
the old has gone, the new has come!

2 Corinthians 5:17

Shake the dust from your past,
and move forward in His promises.

Kay Arthur

Our vision is so limited we can hardly imagine
a love that does not show itself in protection from
suffering. The love of God did not protect
His own Son. He will not necessarily protect us—
not from anything it takes to make us like His Son.
A lot of hammering and chiseling and purifying
by fire will have to go into the process.

Elisabeth Elliot

He was despised and rejected by men,
a man of sorrows, and familiar with suffering.

Isaiah 53:3

In God's economy, whether He is making a flower
or a human soul, nothing ever comes to nothing.
The losses are His way of accomplishing the gains.

Elisabeth Elliot

Many times God gives us a victory
that requires blood, sweat, and tears.

Beth Moore

Jesus loves us with fidelity, purity, constancy,
and passion no matter how imperfect we are.

Stormie Omartian

But God demonstrates his own love for us in this:
While we were still sinners, Christ died for us.

Romans 5:8

…for everyone born of God overcomes the world.
This is the victory that has overcome the world,
even our faith.

1 John 5:4

Suffering is never for nothing.

It is that you and I might be conformed

to the image of Christ.

Elisabeth Elliot

I am not a theologian or a scholar,
but I am very aware of the fact that pain
is necessary to all of us. In my own life, I think
I can honestly say that out of the deepest pain
has come the strongest conviction of the presence
of God and the love of God.

Elisabeth Elliot

Dear friends, do not be surprised at the painful trial
you are suffering, as though something strange
were happening to you. But rejoice that you
participate in the sufferings of Christ, so that
you may be overjoyed when his glory is revealed.

1 Peter 4:12,13

Make the least of all that goes

and the most of all that comes.

Don't regret what is past.

Cherish what you have.

Look forward to all that is to come.

And most important of all, rely moment

by moment on Jesus Christ.

Gigi Graham Tchividjian

...I do not consider myself yet to have taken hold of it. But one thing I do: Forgetting what is behind and straining toward what is ahead, I press on toward the goal to win the prize for which God has called me heavenward in Christ Jesus.

Philippians 3:13,14

Chapter 10
A Journey of Faith

…but the righteous shall live by …faith.

—

Habakkuk 2:4

*R*uth had no idea what the future held, but she had faith in the God Of Israel. After the loss of her husband, father-in-law, and brother-in-law, Ruth was so convinced that the God of Israel was the true God that she told her mother-in-law, *Where you go I will go, and where you stay I will stay. Your people will be my people and your God my God. (Ruth 1:16)*

Perhaps it was her mother-in-law, Naomi, who influenced Ruth to put her faith in God, or God may have visited Ruth in her need, convincing her of His goodness and power. Whatever the source of her motivation, it is clear that Ruth made the correct decision: She placed her faith in God the Creator. As Christians, we should do no less.

The Bible exhorts us to *...fix our eyes on Jesus, the author and perfecter of our faith.... (Hebrews 12:2)* The journey of life is a journey of faith. When we look to Jesus as our Savior and guide, He makes that journey with us, and He makes that journey worthwhile. Let us, then, build our lives on the firmest foundation: faith in the Son and faith in the Father.

Now faith is being sure of what we hope for
and certain of what we do not see.

Hebrews 11:1

I saw it with the eyes of my heart.

Joni Eareckson Tada

Faith means believing in realities that go beyond
sense and sight...being aware of unseen
divine realities all around you.

Joni Eareckson Tada

Faith is not a feeling; it is action.

It is a willed choice.

Elisabeth Elliot

Faith in faith is pointless.
Faith in a living, active God moves mountains.

Beth Moore

…Have faith in the LORD your God
and you will be upheld….

2 Chronicles 20:20

Faith is a strong power, mastering any difficulty
in the strength of the Lord who made
heaven and earth.

Corrie ten Boom

Faith is like a radar that sees through the fog—
it sees the reality of things at a distance that
the human eye cannot see.

Corrie ten Boom

We live by faith, not by sight.

2 Corinthians 5:7

Faith sees the invisible, believes the unbelievable,
and receives the impossible.

Corrie ten Boom

God often uses that small faithfulness
  to accomplish more than the great things
      of which we dream.

Beth Moore

...I tell you the truth, if you have faith as small as
    mustard seed, you can say to this mountain,
    "Move from here to there" and it will move.
      Nothing will be impossible for you.

Jesus
Matthew 17:20,21

Faith in small things has repercussions
  that ripple all the way out. In a huge, dark room
    a little match can light up the place.

Joni Eareckson Tada

Every experience God gives us,
      every person he puts in our lives,
   is the perfect preparation for the future
      that only he can see.

Corrie ten Boom

What is courage? It is the ability to be strong
     in trust, in conviction, in obedience.
 To be courageous is to step out in faith—to trust
    and obey, no matter what.

Kay Arthur

Grace calls you to get up,

throw off your blanket of helplessness

and to move on through life in faith.

Kay Arthur

I have fought the good fight,

I have finished the race,

I have kept the faith.

Now there is in store for me

the crown of righteousness,

which the Lord, the righteous Judge,

will award to me on that day....

2 Timothy 4:7,8

Chapter 11

A Journey of Relationships

I am the vine; you are the branches...
apart from me you can do nothing.

—

Jesus
John 15:5

When life's pilgrimage is at an end, the success of the journey will be judged by the quality of our relationships. Our relationship with God, through Christ, is paramount. And as Christians, we are commanded to love one another; to the extent we do so, the human relationships we cultivate along the way make our lives a cause for celebration.

From the time of birth until we breathe our last breath, many hands tug at us to follow this way and that. When we put our lives in the hands of God, we will rejoice in the abundance that God provides.

Among God's greatest gifts are the gifts of family and friends. If we journey though life with even a few trusted traveling companions, our joys are doubled and our sorrows halved. Devoted, understanding family members and friends are God's blessing to us (as, of course, we are to them).

We invest time and effort in many enterprises in life, and the time we invest in our relationship with God gives the greatest return. Let us commit ourselves to a growing, loving relationship with our Maker, and let us also commit ourselves to ever-growing relationships with our fellow travelers. After all, the journey here on earth is brief, and we are privileged to share that journey with family and friends. They need us, we need them, and we all need God, so let's hold hands, say a prayer, and love each other as long as God gives us life…and then forevermore.

I am the Vine, you are the branches.
When you're joined with me and I with you,
the relation intimate and organic, the harvest
is sure to be abundant.

Jesus
John 15:5 The Message

When we are in a situation where Jesus
is all we have, we soon discover
He is all we really need.

Gigi Graham Tchividjian

You cannot cooperate with Jesus in becoming
what He wants you to become and simultaneously
be what the world desires to make you.
If you would say, "Take the world but give me Jesus,"
then you must deny yourself and take up your cross.
The simple truth is that your "self" must be put
to death in order for you to get to the point
where, for you, to live is Christ. What will it be?
The world and you, or Jesus and you?
You do have a choice to make.

Kay Arthur

No one can serve two masters.
Either he will hate the one and love the other,
or he will be devoted to the one
and despise the other.

Jesus
Matthew 6:24

I am convinced our hearts are not healthy
until they have been satisfied by the only
completely healthy love that exists:
the love of God, Himself.

Beth Moore

For God so loved the world that he gave his one
and only Son, that whoever believes in Him
shall not perish but have eternal life.

John 3:16

God's glorious, incomprehensible desire
         is to meet with humans.

Beth Moore

God created us, not because He needed us,
         but because He wanted us.
The act was based on the pleasure of His will.

Beth Moore

Delighting thyself in the Lord is the sudden realization that He has become the desire of your heart.

Beth Moore

A good marriage is the union of two forgivers.

Ruth Graham

The love life of the Christian is a crucial battleground.
There, if nowhere else, it will be determined who
is Lord—the world, the self and the devil,
or the Lord Christ.

Elisabeth Elliot

We've grown to be one soul—two parts;
our lives are so intertwined that when some passion
stirs your heart, I feel the quake in mine.

Gloria Gaither

I will find in every person that facet
of the Lord's loveliness that only
he or she can uniquely reflect.

Joni Eareckson Tada

A friend loves at all times....

Proverbs 17:17

Line by line, moment by moment,
    special times are etched into our memories
      in the permanent ink of everlasting love
        in our relationships.

Gloria Gaither

In friendship, God opens your eyes
    to the glories of Himself.

Joni Eareckson Tada

No matter how efficient, smart, or independent
we happen to think ourselves to be, sooner or later
we run into a "brick wall" that our intelligence
or experience cannot handle for us. We can fake it,
avoid it, or blunder through it. But a better solution
would be to find someone who has walked that way
before and has gained wisdom from experience.

Gloria Gaither

We long to find someone who has been
where we've been who shares our fragile skies,
who sees our sunsets with the same shades of blue.

Beth Moore

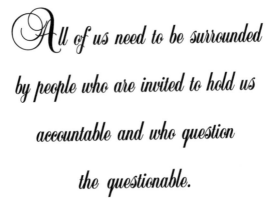

All of us need to be surrounded
by people who are invited to hold us
accountable and who question
the questionable.

Beth Moore

Celebrate God all day, every day.

I mean, revel in him!

Paul
Philippians 4:4 The Message

Spiritual Resources available to you from LifeWay Clubs and Plans

A Heart Like His Devotional Journal
by Beth Moore

Based on her best-selling book, this 160 page journal features inspirational thoughts and journaling questions that will bring you closer to the heart of God.

080543528X   Reg. $14.99   **Sale $11.99**

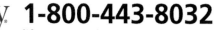

Beth Moore is available to you from LifeWay Clubs and Plans

Feathers from My Nest
A Mother's Reflections
by Beth Moore

Beth Moore is widely known and respected as an engaging and effective speaker, Bible teacher, and best-selling author. *Feathers from My Nest* reveals a more contemplative and personal side of Beth, very much in the spirit of her *Things Pondered*.

Feathers from My Nest is a collection of vignettes, as Beth reflects on items belonging to her daughters who have left the nest for college. As she ponders each item, rich in memories, Beth draws from it spiritual significance.

This books not only gently tugs on the sentimental heartstrings of parents, it also reminds us all of the gift of grace children offer our lives everyday.

0805424644   Reg. $14.99   **Sale $11.99**